# Fresh and Sophisticated

Enjoy

love

Claire Maguire

# Fresh and Sophisticated
## The Art of Radiant Eating

## Claire Maguire

Raw Horizons Retreat
at Split Farthing Hall
www.rawhorizons.co.uk

Photography by Sam Miller Gott

Dr Claire Maguire is the UK's leading transformational wellbeing coach. She runs the much loved and successful Raw Horizons Retreat at Split Farthing Hall in North Yorkshire where women come to reflect, re-energise, evolve and have a great time. She has developed her signature wellbeing programmes which cover areas such as confidence, self-esteem, passion, stress management, vitality, food relationship and how to nourish your body.

Claire's philosophy is that food is the foundation of becoming a radiant woman and uses her skills to create beautiful uplifting food to nourish her guests. She has been featured in many national magazines including Woman & Home and Psychologies.

As well as an avid food lover, Claire loves to practice Kundalini yoga, spend time dancing and engaging with an audience. She lives in North Yorkshire with her two beautiful daughters and numerous pets.

First published in the United Kingdom in 2014
Revised edition published in the United Kingdom 2017

Published by Raw Horizons Limited
Split Farthing Hall
Bagby
Thirsk
North Yorkshire
YO7 2AF
United Kingdom
www.rawhorizons.com

ISBN 978-0-90-477570-9

A CIP catalogue record for this book is available from the British Library.

Printed and bound in the United Kingdom by GH Smith & Son.

Designer, Food Stylist, Prop Stylist and Photographer: Sam Miller Gott
Editors: Andrea Maguire, Angela Maguire, Michael Maguire and Sam Miller Gott

Charlotte Morrison's work can be found on pages 15, 19, 23, 27, 46, 60, 64 and 67.
You can find Charlotte's beautiful work at www.charlotte-morrison.co.uk.

# Acknowledgements

The biggest heartfelt thank you that I can give is to my children, Amy and Zoe, who have to listen to me constantly going on about spinach! They are awesome, generous, helpful and total superstars and to them this book is dedicated.

Whilst on the mention of family, the whole reason this book has seen the light of day is due to the support, belief and organisational skills of my Dad and Andrea, my step-mum. They have stood by me and my conviction that the guests on a retreat at Split Farthing Hall have to eat raw food and encouraged me to turn my passions into a business. Thank you for letting me do my funky stuff in the kitchen. And, thank you to my Mum who did an amazing job editing this book and generously lending some of her beautiful dishes that are seen throughout. Thank you for being there when I need to let off steam and talk.

Of course, as is the way, no book is ever done by just one person and this book is no exception. There have been numerous people along the way that have nudged me to put my recipes into a book. It has been a long process of people asking and me putting it off until the wonderful Sam Miller Gott stepped into my life. Sam sunk her teeth into this project and gave me the motivation I needed. We had a fabulous, crazy, non-stop time making and photographing all my recipes. It is a week I will treasure forever. The resulting photographs are truly stunning, capturing completely the essence of my food. Thank you for returning to design, edit and ensuring the book was finished!

I have to give a big thanks to Emma Sutton, who has helped me in the kitchen over these last few months and has made me laugh so much and bought some much needed light relief from the craziness of writing this book. Your attitude to life is delightful.

Thank you to Charlotte Morrison for the loan of her gorgeous hand-made ceramics. My thanks also go to Clive Anderson of Mount Pleasant Farm, Balk for supplying the delicious fresh fruit and vegetables, Dales of Thirsk for lending us the lovely marble countertops and Chris Trenholme for helping to move them around!

To all those who have helped out at Split Farthing Hall over the years: Lisa, Rebecca, Sol, Laura and Lindsey, you've all played your part and provided me with laughter, care and fun.

And of course I have to thank all the guests who have been on our retreats at Raw Horizons. Without you this book would never have been created. Thank you for enjoying my food, asking for the recipes, being open, honest, having great conversations and for being fabulous even when you were in the throes of cravings! I've loved feeding every one of you.

# Contents

# Introduction

I will start by saying what I always say to guests on our retreats at Split Farthing Hall- I am not a fanatical raw vegan and I have no desire to turn you into one. Yet this book and the food I feed to my guests on retreats is all raw vegan.

So why?

For me, raw food is amazing. I know this is not going to sound at all scientific and considering my background as a doctor of Biochemistry, this flies in the face of all I learnt... raw food has a certain magic in it! Yes, it sounds wacky but when I eat raw food, the magic that I mention works within your body to make you feel amazing. It makes you feel radiant and alive. It helps to give you focus and clarity. Raw food can literally transform you on a mind, body and soul level. Big claims to make for what is ultimately just food. Yet eating is believing.

I know that it can be challenging to eat all raw as it's far removed from our normal way of eating. The reality is that in your day-to-day life it isn't what I would expect you to do. On our retreats, however, I give my guests the opportunity to immerse themselves in this different way of eating. For sure, there can be initial symptoms of physical detox but the one thing I notice over and over again is the ladies look radiant when they leave, they feel uplifted and happy. I know this is a combination of all the things going on whilst on my retreat which creates this state but the food is the foundation of it all.

I'm not here though to say you must eat raw food for 'this' nutrient or 'that' health reason. That is not my aim when I feed people. My true desire is for people to embrace raw food as a cuisine they can enjoy and this way of eating to be accepted as part of their food lifestyle. Ultimately, I would love raw food to be seen as a delicious accompaniment to life.

As you start to eat more raw food, notice your body and how it feels. Take note of what shifts you observe within yourself: about your energy, your shape, your skin, your mind, your clarity, your creativity and see your radiance shine through. For when you can feel that change within you, then you make the decision that you will embrace a new way of eating. There is nobody who can say what you should or should not eat. When people lay down the rules about what to eat, guess what? The majority of us rebel against it, crave all sorts and sabotage all our best-laid intentions. Truly, it has to come from within you. You have to accept what you want to eat for yourself and how you are going to go about it.

I am opening up the opportunity of new recipes for you to try and discover the effect they have within you. When you take a moment to explore your relationship with food then you can make choices that reflect your needs. Raw food will bring up your emotions and if your usual way to deal with any emotional situation is by eating, then stripping away your normal coping mechanism will mean you have to face that emotion and let it go. This can be tough but so rewarding. It is the one aspect I do love about eating raw food and when I want to experience some level of personal growth I increase my intake of raw food.

In fact, raw food has been pivotal in my own life, facilitating personal transformation. I first encountered raw food as a lifestyle concept way of eating back in the summer of 2007. I'm not sure how I stumbled upon it. I remember reading a blog which inspired me to try and create some raw food dishes. I had no preconceived ideas, no expectations other than trying a new way of making food. I have always loved being in the kitchen and I enjoyed making these new recipes. I found it fun experimenting and discovering new foods. Yet something else happened! I found an inner strength, a clarity, a sexy sassiness that sparked off a passion in me to start a new life. I left a turbulent marriage and embarked on a new path. I embraced raw food and trained as a raw food coach which led to me setting up a business called The Raw Bombshell which had as its premise using raw food to connect with the woman you truly are.

I loved this period of growth, expansion, connection and pure radiance that raw food gave to me.

Yet in May 2009, I discovered I had breast cancer. Initially I wasn't fazed by the diagnosis and thought I could cure myself. But three months after the diagnosis I discovered it had spread to the lymph nodes. For me, I knew my path was medical treatment. During this period raw food didn't appeal, it made me feel worse if truth be known. However, I was pulled back by a desire to eat raw during radiotherapy. It was as if my body had decided it wanted to feel the raw magic. So I embraced raw food again, although never as fanatically as before! I do believe that eating a high proportion of raw food helped me to recover quickly, easily and feel good about myself.

From that point on, raw food has always been a part of my everyday diet. I love the creativity of it, the simplicity of it and most of all I love the way it shapes my body and energises my mind. To me raw food is the basis to the Art of Radiant Eating.

I do hope that this recipe book will inspire you to create raw food dishes, to see how beautiful this way of eating is, to love all the fresh flavours and to enjoy the sophistication within each dish.

**How to use the book:**

- It is my hope this book will allow you to explore raw recipes and how you can incorporate eating raw into your everyday life. This book is not, as I said, a bid to turn you into a raw vegan! Feel free to add meat, eggs, etc. to any of the dishes or if you're cooking for your family and want to cater more to their tastes. Bear in mind any allergies or intolerances, especially if using ingredients for the first time.

- Most recipes include a notes section. This allows you the space to adapt the recipe to your tastes, add any other yummy bits or adjust for your kitchen equipment.

- Soaking, sprouting, fermenting, marinating, dehydrating, refrigerating and freezing times are not to the minute. They are not time critical as there's nothing to burn in the oven!

- For recipes that use a dehydrator, a handy clock symbol next to the page number lets you know you'll need to allow for dehydrating time.

 Indicates required dehydrating      Indicates optional dehydrating

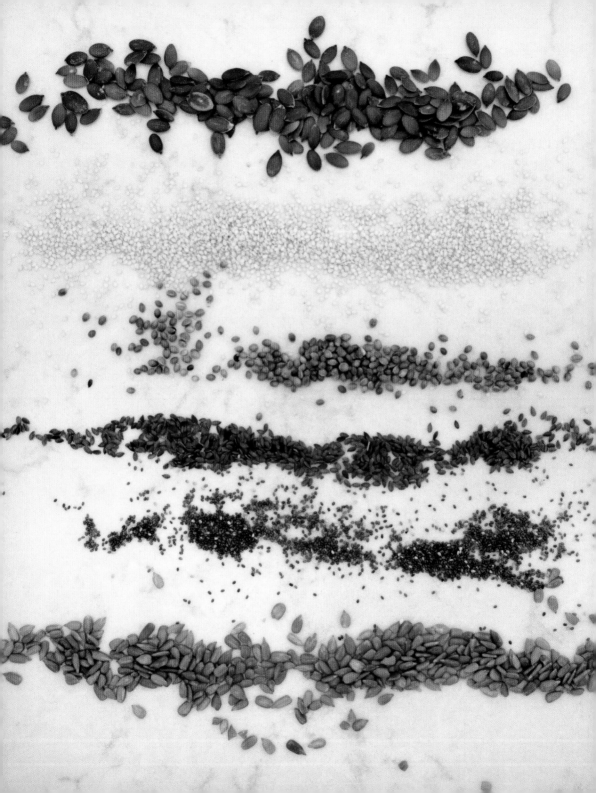

# Breakfast

I love breakfast. On our retreats at Split Farthing Hall everyone is very ready to eat breakfast after our morning Kundalini yoga. The breakfasts that you find here certainly give you the satisfaction of a full tummy and provide great energy to start your day.

I have created the breakfasts in this section to resemble what you may already be eating – a bowl of something with milk! The milk I use is usually almond milk which I always make myself and to me tastes so much nicer than cows' milk.

Within this section you will find a raw porridge which is often preferred by many of my guests to cooked porridge and is so easy to prepare. There are cereal dishes made with buckwheat and one which turns the milk chocolate; a raw version of toast; muesli; granola and my all-time favourite breakfast: chia pudding. Chia seeds are becoming more popular and can now be found easily in the big supermarkets.

Try one of these breakfasts with a smoothie or juice and see what difference it makes to your morning. Ask yourself how do I feel straight after eating it, is my energy high, does my tummy feel content? Then ask yourself these questions a couple of hours later. This is my way of consistently observing and finding out which foods really serve my body to make me look and feel radiant.

# Blackberry Chia Pudding

50g blackberries
200ml almond milk (see pg 26)
1 Medjool date
30g chia seeds

Place the blackberries, pitted date and almond milk in a blender and blend to make a beautiful purple milk.

Add half of the milk to the chia seeds and leave them to soak for 30 minutes. You will find the chia absorbs all of the milk, swells up and becomes a solid consistency. This is fine.

Add the rest of the blackberry almond milk just before serving and with a spoon, break up all of the chia to create a more smooth consistency.

Place in breakfast bowls and top with fresh berries or fruit. Can also be sweetened to taste by drizzling honey over the top.

Chia pudding has to be one of my all-time favourite breakfasts and one I eat on a very regular basis. It does have a strange consistency, which can be strange the first time, however, the flavour is mild and pleasant plus it does you the world of good.

**Soaking Time:** 30 minutes
**Storage:** Refrigerate in an airtight container for up to 3 days  **Serves:** 2
**Tip:** You can also soak the chia with any nut milk without blackberries blended in.

Notes

# Ginger Crispies

100g buckwheaties
  (see page 132)
50g shelled hemp seeds
1 tbsp maca powder

2 tbsp coconut oil
3 tbsp agave nectar
¼ tsp ground ginger

In a bowl add the buckwheaties and shelled hemp seeds.

In a bain marie melt the coconut oil. You will find the coconut oil melts quickly. Coconut oil is liquid at warm temperatures and solid at cooler ones, so you know you are having great weather when you don't have to melt the coconut oil!

To the melted coconut oil add the maca powder, agave nectar and ginger. Whisk together until they are well combined.

Add this liquid mixture to the buckwheaties and hemp seeds. Toss them together so they are evenly coated.

Spread out onto a Paraflexx sheet and dehydrate overnight.

As there is coconut oil in the mixture you will find that the mixture doesn't come out crispy the next morning. Put into the refrigerator to crisp up.

Serve with a nut milk and fresh fruit.

**Dehydration Time:** Overnight
**Storage:** Refrigerate for up to 2 weeks  **Serves:** 4 (or 2 large portions)
**Tip:** Add more ginger or fresh ginger if you like more bite to your breakfast.

Notes

# Muesli with Cashew Yoghurt

## Cashew Yoghurt

   100g cashews
   5 probiotic capsules
   150ml water

Add the cashews to a blender and blend with the water until smooth. Open up the probiotic capsules and sprinkle the powder into the mixture (discard the shell). Pulse very quickly to blend in. You could just stir it in if you prefer.

Set aside somewhere warm and leave overnight. The next day there will be bubbles on the surface and the mixture will have slightly separated. Just give it a quick stir.

## Muesli

   100g fine milled oats
   30g sesame seeds
   20g dried blueberries
   20g dried cherries
   ½ tsp cinnamon
   Pinch of salt
   1 apple

Put the dry ingredients into a bowl and fold through. Just before serving, juice the apple and mix into the dry mixture. This will help to soften the muesli. You are wanting to just slightly moisten the muesli as this is best served with a dryish consistency.

To serve put the muesli mixture to a bowl and top with yoghurt.

**Fermentation Time:** Overnight
**Storage:** Store the cashew yoghurt in the fridge for up to two days **Serves:** 2
**Tip:** You can use store-bought apple juice instead of juicing an apple if you prefer.

Notes

# "Toast" with Berries

250g flax seeds (linseeds)
100g sunflower seeds
50g chia seeds
3 tbsp psyllium husks

1 tbsp cinnamon
3 tbsp honey
100ml water
½ tsp salt

Put flax seeds into a bowl and cover with water. Leave to soak for 1 hour. The flax will absorb the water and become gloopy. Pour this into a food processor along with all the other ingredients and mix together for 2 minutes. The flax seeds will not beak down and will stay whole, which is fine.

Spread out the resulting mixture, which will have the consistency of thick dough, onto a Paraflexx sheet with a spatula. There will be enough mixture for 2 trays. Place in the dehydrator overnight.

The next morning peel off the flax mixture and place upside down onto another Paraflexx sheet. Put back in the dehydrator for a further 6 hours.

The final mixture will still be flexible and not brittle so use scissors to cut the flax mixture into triangles and serve with fruit and/or honey. If you wish to change up your bacon sandwich, use this toast to replace the bread!

**Dehydration Time:** 18 hours
**Storage:** Refrigerate in an airtight container for up to 1 month  **Makes:** 36 pieces
**Tip:** Make in bulk so you always have some for when you need something substantial to eat.

Notes

# Bircher Muesli with Brazil Nut Milk

## Brazil Nut Milk

50g Brazil nuts
150ml water
1 Medjool date

Add Brazil nuts to the blender with the pitted date and water, blend for 2 minutes.

There is no need to strain the milk even though it's not completely smooth. It adds texture to the breakfast.

If you prefer a smoother milk you can strain it with a nut milk bag. Brazil nut milk can have a foamy consistency.

## Bircher Muesli

100g oats
1 apple

Cover the oats with the Brazil nut milk and put to one side either overnight or for a minimum of 30 minutes. The oats will absorb the milk.

Grate the apple just before serving and stir into the oats. You can add more milk if you feel it is too dry.

Top with fresh berries, fruit and/or seeds. Best eaten fresh.

**Soaking Time:** 30 minutes - overnight
**Storage:** The milk will keep in the refrigerator for up to 4 days  **Serves:** 2
**Tip:** You can use any nut milk in place of Brazil nut milk.

Notes

# Fruit & Nut Granola

250g hazelnuts
100g raisins
100g dried blueberries

100g pecans
3 large or 4 small apples

Add nuts and dried fruit to a food processor. Quarter the apples, remove the core, and add to the food processor. Pulse together to chop the nuts and fruit to small pieces and apple is mixed into the fruit and nut mixture. This will make a wet mixture.

Spread out onto a Paraflexx sheet and place into the dehydrator overnight.

In the morning flip onto another Paraflexx sheet and dry for a further 6 hours. Break into pieces, serve with a nut milk of your choice and top with raspberries.

You can also drizzle honey over the top as no extra sweetener has been added to the recipe.

**Dehydration Time:** 18 hours
**Storage:** Refrigerate for up to 1 month  **Makes:** 550g final weight
**Tip:** If you don't have a dehydrator you can place the mixture in a cool oven for 2 hours or until dry. You can swap dried blueberries for goji berries.

Notes

# Dreamy Porridge with Blueberries & Almond Milk

## Almond Milk

250g almonds
2 Medjool dates
2 litres water (approx)

Put the almonds in a bowl, cover with water and soak overnight. Drain off water and rinse well in cold water. Place them in a blender with the pitted dates and blend with 1 litre of water.

Empty the mixture into a muslin bag and gently squeeze all the "milk" from the bag. Add water to the "milk" to bring to 2 litres.

You can use different nuts to make different tasting milks.

## Porridge

100g jumbo porridge oats
100g blueberries

Cover the oats with water and add the blueberries. Leave to soak overnight. Drain off water but don't rinse the oats. You will find the oats are softened to resemble porridge and the blueberries will be plump.

Spoon into bowls and pour almond milk over the top. This dish is not sweet, so you can drizzle honey over the top. Also top with dried fruits, nuts plus superfoods such as cacao nibs for a breakfast that will keep you raring to go all morning. Best eaten fresh.

**Soaking Time:** Overnight  **Storage:** Refrigerate milk for up to 3 days  **Serves:** 2
**Tip:** The leftover almond pulp can be either used like almond meal or composted. The almond milk does not have to be strained, it's just thicker with more texture.

Notes

# Cinnamon & Seed Granola

100g sunflower seeds
150g pumpkin seeds
50g whole hemp seeds
100g goji berries

2 tsp cinnamon
1 tsp nutmeg
4 tbsp honey
250g banana (peeled weight)

Add all the seeds and goji berries to a food processor, sprinkle in the cinnamon and, as I like to use whole nutmeg, grate the nutmeg directly into the bowl. Add the honey and banana to the food processor and pulse until all mixed together and the banana has blended into the seed mixture.

Spread out onto a Paraflexx sheet and place into the dehydrator overnight. The next morning, flip the granola onto another Paraflexx sheet and dry for a further 6 hours.

Break into pieces, pour over your choice of nut milk and serve with mulberries.

**Dehydration Time:** 18 hours
**Storage:** Refrigerate for up to 1 month **Makes:** 500g final weight
**Tip:** As this recipe will make more than one breakfast, store the remaining in the refrigerator.

Notes

# Chocolate Crème in Papaya

50g macadamia nuts
1 tbsp cacao powder
1/2 tbsp maca powder
1/3 tbsp agave nectar
2 tbsp water
1 papaya

To make the chocolate crème, add the macadamia nuts with the cacao, maca, agave nectar and water to a small food processor. As you're not making a big quantity, it won't mix together well in a large food processor, so I usually use a hand held one.

Pulse together so the nuts break down and form a chocolate crème with the other ingredients. However, don't pulse for too long as you don't want a smooth paste.

This tastes much better with the macadamias in large pieces. It's just good to have the crunch!

Cut the papaya in half and scoop out the seeds.

Spoon the chocolate crème mix into the space created by removing the seeds.

Eat immediately for a decadent and indulgent breakfast.

**Preparation Time:** 20 minutes  **Serves:** 2 or just for you!
**Tip:** Ladies, this is a great breakfast to have when you feel PMT striking as that time of the month is perfect for eating chocolate and maca.

Notes

# Choco Clusters

200g buckwheat
1 tbsp honey
4 Medjool dates
25g cacao nibs
25g cacao powder

1 tsp vanilla powder
Salt to season
Tiny piece of dried
   chipotle chilli

Soak the buckwheat first by placing the dried buckwheat in a bowl, cover with water and leave overnight. Drain the next day and rinse well with water.

Add the soaked buckwheat to a food processor along with all the other ingredients making sure to pit the dates. Pulse for a minute to bind the mixture together but not to turn it into a paste as you still want the texture of the buckwheat.

With your hands take small pieces of the buckwheat mixture and sprinkle it out onto a Paraflexx sheet so it forms clusters. Put into the dehydrator over-night.

Serve with a nut milk of your choice and banana.

**Dehydration Time:** Overnight
**Storage:** Refrigerate for up to 1 month in an airtight container **Serves:** 2
**Tip:** You can double or triple this recipe.

Notes

# Lunch

I keep lunches on our retreats fresh and simple. There is often a strong slant on including greens in a lunch recipe. For me, greens are the focus for being radiant, for feeling good and happy in your body. I eat them often and if I feel out of balance with my body the first question I ask myself is, "Have I been eating my greens?" and you know, usually I haven't. To get back to feeling good, I eat greens! I guess grandma was right when she told us to eat your greens to get fit and strong... and it certainly worked for Popeye!

There is versatility with the lunch section as you can take the recipes and really adapt them to whatever ingredients you have in your kitchen and what you fancy. For example, the stir unfry can be made with all the vegetables I suggest or you can vary it by omitting some of the suggestions and adding what you like, plus you can add meat, fish or egg and serve it with noodles. My desire, is for you to add more raw food into your everyday life and to see raw cuisine as exciting. It doesn't have to be an all or nothing approach.

The lunch recipes on the whole are quick to prepare, the exception being the raw "BLT" which is super easy but does have dehydration time. The dishes also taste great when left to marinate for a period of time as the flavours mingle together. Hence you can easily make one of these recipes and take it to work for lunch.

# Broad Bean Salad in Lemon & Sage

200g broad beans
  (fresh or frozen)
2 large spring onions
1 apple
2 cloves of garlic
½ lemon

1 tbsp olive oil
Small handful of sage
100g bunch of asparagus
Salt and pepper to taste
Mixed salad leaves

If you are using fresh broad beans, shell the beans and weigh out 200 grams. Alternatively, if you are using frozen broad beans defrost them before using. In either case, add the beans to a bowl. Chop the spring onions finely and add to the broad beans along with the apple, cored and chopped into small pieces.

Crush the garlic and put in another bowl along with the juice of the lemon, olive oil and the finely chopped sage.

Mix together well with a fork to make the dressing and pour over the bean mixture.

Remove the tips from the asparagus and set to one side. Chop the remainder of the asparagus spears into small pieces and stir through the bean mixture. Season with salt and pepper.

Serve on mixed salad leaves and decorate with the asparagus tips. Best eaten fresh.

**Preparation Time:** 15 minutes  **Serves:** 2
**Tip:** This salad is lovely with chopped hard boiled egg, Parma ham and/or artichokes.

Notes

# Cucumber Subs with Mango Chutney

## Cucumber Subs

1 cucumber
100g pumpkin seeds
40g dried apricots
2 tsp caraway seeds

Cut the cucumber in half crossways and scoop out the seeds. I find using a grapefruit knife the easiest way to do this. Discard the seeds.

Put the pumpkin seeds, dried apricots and caraway seeds into a food processor and mix together until the seeds and fruit form a sticky mixture. Using a teaspoon, take some of this mixture and stuff it into the cucumber. Repeat until the cucumber is full. Chill until needed.

## Mango Chutney

1 mango
½ tsp cayenne pepper
½ tsp coriander seeds

Peel the mango and cut the fruit off the stone.

Add the mango fruit to a blender with the cayenne pepper and coriander seeds. Pulse for about 10 seconds as you still want the mango to be chunky.

Serve by wrapping the end of the cucumber with a napkin and dip the other end into the chutney for each bite.

**Preparation Time:** 20 minutes
**Storage:** Refrigerate chutney for up to 3 days  **Serves:** 2
**Tip:** You can use the pumpkin seed mixture to stuff into peppers instead.

Notes

# Broccoli in a Hoisin Style Sauce

650g broccoli
200g mushrooms
5 spring onions
50g pecans
2 tbsp sesame seeds
3 tbsp tamari

3 tbsp rapeseed oil
½ tbsp agave nectar
2 tsp maca powder
1 tsp rice wine vinegar
Splash of Tabasco

Chop the large stalk off the broccoli and discard, then cut the head of broccoli into small florets and place in a bowl.

Chop the mushrooms into chunks and the spring onions into small pieces and add to the bowl of broccoli.

Break the pecan nuts into pieces and add to the vegetables along with the sesame seeds.

In another bowl, add tamari, rapeseed oil, agave nectar, maca powder, rice wine vinegar and a splash of Tabasco. Beat together with a fork to make the hoisin style sauce. Rub this sauce into the vegetable mixture with your hands.

Put the broccoli mixture onto a Paraflexx sheet and dehydrate for 4 hours. Serve warm.

**Dehydration Time:** 4 hours
**Note:** You can eat this dish without dehydrating the broccoli **Serves: 2**
**Tip:** Add beansprouts, bamboo shoots and water chestnuts after dehydrating.

Notes

# Raw "BLT" on Walnut Bread Rolls

## The "Bacon" Part

1 aubergine
2 tbsp rapeseed oil
2 tbsp tamari
1 tsp meat rub of your choice

Cut the aubergine length ways into thin strips. Mix the oil, tamari and meat rub together in a small bowl and pour over the aubergine. Marinate for 30 minutes. Put the aubergine onto a dehydrator tray and dehydrate overnight.

## The Extras

1 beef tomato
1 little gem lettuce
1 avocado
English mustard

Mash avocado onto half a bread roll, top with a slice of tomato, add some aubergine pieces and a lettuce leaf. Spread some mustard onto the other half of the bread roll and put on top.

## Walnut Bread

150g walnuts
100g pumpkin seeds
200g courgette
100g onion
2 tsp ground coriander
2 tbsp milled flax/
  goji berry mix
5 tbsp psyllium husks
1 tbsp tamari

Grind the walnuts and pumpkin seeds together in a food processor until you have a mixture that resembles fine bread crumbs. Empty this mixture into a bowl. Put the courgettes and onion in to the food processor and pulse to a purée and add to the dry walnut mixture.

Stir in the remaining ingredients, season with salt and pepper and shape the mixture into 6 small bread roll shapes. Place into the dehydrator overnight. The next morning, cut the rolls in half and return to the dehydrator for a further 6 hours.

**Dehydration Time:** 18 hours  **Makes:** 6 bread rolls
**Tip:** Store the unused "bacon" and bread rolls in the refrigerator for another time for up to 5 days.

# Kale Salad

100g kale
1 avocado
½ tsp salt
Squeeze of lemon
40g fennel

1 tbsp dried cranberries
2 tbsp pistachios
1 conference pear
2 tbsp capers
85g olives

Tear the kale into small pieces, removing the stalk from the kale leaves as they are too woody for this recipe. Place remaining leaves in a bowl.

Cut the avocado in half, remove the pit and discard. Spoon out the soft flesh into the bowl and using your hands massage the avocado into the kale along with the salt and a squeeze of lemon. The lemon is used more to stop the avocado from discolouring rather than for taste.

Set the kale to one side to soften, you can leave it for 30 minutes up to 3 hours.

Just before eating, finely chop the fennel and pear and add to the kale mixture. Add in the dried cranberries, pistachios, capers and olives. Toss together and serve immediately.

This is a great salad for winter when kale is in season. It is strong and robust so can carry flavours and textures well.

**Marinating Time:** 30 minutes - 3 hours **Serves:** 2
**Tip:** Play with the basic kale salad (the avocado and salt massaged in) by adding any ingredients you fancy. I also like pomegranate seeds, sun dried tomatoes, grapes and, when you can find it, samphire.

Notes

# Green Salad in Thai Style Dressing

## Thai Style Dressing

¼ red jalapeño chilli pepper
1 tbsp tamarind concentrate
1 tsp coriander seeds
1 Medjool date
1 tbsp tamari
50ml water

Put the jalapeño, tamarind, coriander seeds, pitted date, tamari and water into a blender and blend until smooth. This is your Thai style dressing.

## Salad

100g mixed baby salad leaves
2 spring onions
200g pak choi
6 baby sweetcorn
Big handful of beansprouts
50g water chestnuts
Handful of coriander leaves
50g roasted peanuts

To make the salad, add the salad leaves to a bowl. Finely shred the pak choi and add to bowl. Chop the sweetcorn and spring onions into small rounds then also add to the bowl. Throw in the beansprouts, water chestnuts and add the dressing.

Toss well and leave to marinate for 30 mins. The salad leaves will wilt slightly which is great for this dish. Too often we think we have to eat lettuce all crisp and fresh but every now and again it's good to have a different texture.

**To Serve:** Plate up the salad and sprinkle over the coriander leaves and peanuts.
**Preparation Time:** 10 minutes  **Serves:** 2
**Tip:** You can make extra dressing by doubling the quantities and then pouring more over the top to taste.

# Stir Unfry with Firecrackers

## Firecrackers

- 250g flax seeds
- 400ml water
- 4 tbsp tamari sauce
- 30g fresh coriander
- 1 large chilli

Cover the flax seeds with water and soak for 2 hours. The flax seeds will absorb the water and become gloopy. Pour the mixture into a food processor. Add the tamari, coriander and chilli and blend until finely chopped although the flax seed will remain whole.

Pour the mixture out onto a Paraflexx sheet and spread evenly. Place into the dehydrator overnight. Then flip onto another Paraflexx sheet and dry for a further 6 hours or until crispy. Break into pieces.

## Stir Unfry

- 100g red pepper
- 50g mange tout
- 100g sugar snap peas
- 100g carrot
- 100g beansprouts
- 200g pineapple
- 20g bamboo shoots
- ½ orange
- 1 tsp Chinese five spice powder
- 1 tbsp rapeseed oil
- ½ tbsp honey

Julienne the red pepper, mange tout and carrot. Chop the sugar snap peas into small pieces and dice the pineapple. Put all in a bowl with the beansprouts and bamboo shoots. In another bowl, add the juice of the orange and remaining ingredients. Mix well together and pour over the vegetable mixture.

**Dehydration Time:** 18 hours
**Note:** You can have the unfry without the crackers for a quick meal  **Serves:** 2
**Tip:** You can serve this with strips of cooked chicken and noodles.

Notes

# Caesar Salad with Garlic Croutons

## Caesar Salad

2 romaine lettuce heads
6 asparagus spears
75g cashews
2 tbsp capers
1 tsp Dijon mustard
Big pinch of salt
100ml water

Rip the lettuce up with your hands and add to a bowl.

Put the cashews, capers, Dijon mustard, salt and water into a blender. Blend until smooth. I recommend making the dressing before needed and leave to stand in the refrigerator for up to 8 hours. This allows the flavours to mingle and the sauce to thicken to a creamy consistency.

## Garlic Croutons

300g soaked and sprouted buckwheat (weigh this out after soaking)
1 tbsp olive oil
1 tsp salt
1 lemon
3 tsp garlic granules
Pepper
100ml water

Add all the ingredients into a food processor. Mix until you have a runny and smooth consistency. It will be very runny! Pour onto a Paraflexx sheet. Dehydrate overnight, then flip over and dehydrate for a further 4 hours or until completely dry. They will break easily and be crumbly, this is fine.

**To Serve:** To make the Caesar salad, pour the dressing over the lettuce and mix together. Sprinkle a couple of handfuls of the garlic croutons (you will have made more than you need) onto the lettuce and gently toss. Place asparagus spears to decorate and serve. **Note:** Garlic croutons are optional **Dehydration Time:** 16 hours **Storage:** Refrigerate the extra croutons for up to 1 month **Serves:** 2
**Tip:** You can turn this into a Waldorf salad by swapping the croutons for celery, apple and walnuts. Store the extra garlic croutons in the fridge for use later.

# Jewelled "Couscous"

150g sunflower seeds
1 tsp allspice powder
½ tsp turmeric
1 tsp ground cumin
1 tsp ground ginger
½ orange (medium)

1 tbsp olive oil
50g dried apricots
50g green beans
50g yellow pepper
100g pomegranate seeds
Lettuce leaves

Add the sunflower seeds, allspice powder, turmeric, cumin and ginger to a food processor and pulse until the seeds resemble bread crumbs. This is the "couscous"! Add in the juice and rind from the orange, the olive oil and add salt and pepper to taste. Pulse the food processor to quickly mix.

Chop the dried apricots, green beans and yellow pepper into small chunks and stir through the sunflower seed mixture.

Serve over lettuce leaves and sprinkle pomegranate seeds over the top.

**Preparation Time:** 15 minutes
**Storage:** The "couscous" will keep for up to a week in the refrigerator **Serves:** 2
**Tip:** Add the fruit and vegetables when you are ready to serve. You can try adding raisins as well.

Notes

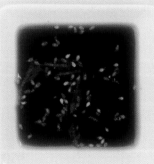

# Sunflower Sushi with Pickled Cabbage

## Sunflower Seed "Rice"

100g sunflower seeds
50ml water
1 tbsp sushi rice seasoning

To make the "rice", pulse together the sunflower seeds with the water and sushi rice seasoning until it resembles a rice texture. Put to one side, whilst you julienne your chosen ingredients as needed.

## Sushi & Filling

2 nori sushi sheets
Small bowl of water
Choose 3 or 4 items from:
Avocado - Pepper - Carrot - Chives
Cucumber - Beansprouts
Pea Shoots – Mushroom - Radish

To assemble your sushi, take one nori sheet and place it shiny side down on a mat. Spread the sunflower seed rice thinly over the nori, leaving the edge furthest away from you, about one inch, uncovered. Add a thin strip of your chosen fillings across the nori sheet, about 1/3 of the way from the edge closest to you. To roll, take the edge closest to you and carefully roll over the filling and firmly tucking and rolling. Moisten the exposed edge of the nori sheet with water and then carry on rolling. You will have made a long tube. Slice the tube into 7 pieces. Repeat with the second nori sheet.

## Dipping Sauce

400g tomato
2 tbsp tamari
1 tbsp rice wine vinegar
1 tsp sesame seeds
Rind of 1 lemon

Make the dipping sauce by adding tamari, rice wine vinegar, sesame seeds and lemon rind together. Place in a small dish ready for dipping your sushi pieces.

## Pickled Cabbage

400g red cabbage
2 tbsp rice wine vinegar
1 tbsp white wine vinegar
1 tsp salt

Shred the red cabbage finely, toss in the vinegars and salt. Place a salad bowl and serve.

**Preparation Time:** 30 minutes  **Serves:** 2
**Tip:** You can serve with pickled ginger and wasabi too. Other sushi fillings include cooked chicken, cooked prawn and smoked salmon. You can also use a white cabbage instead of red for the pickled cabbage salad.

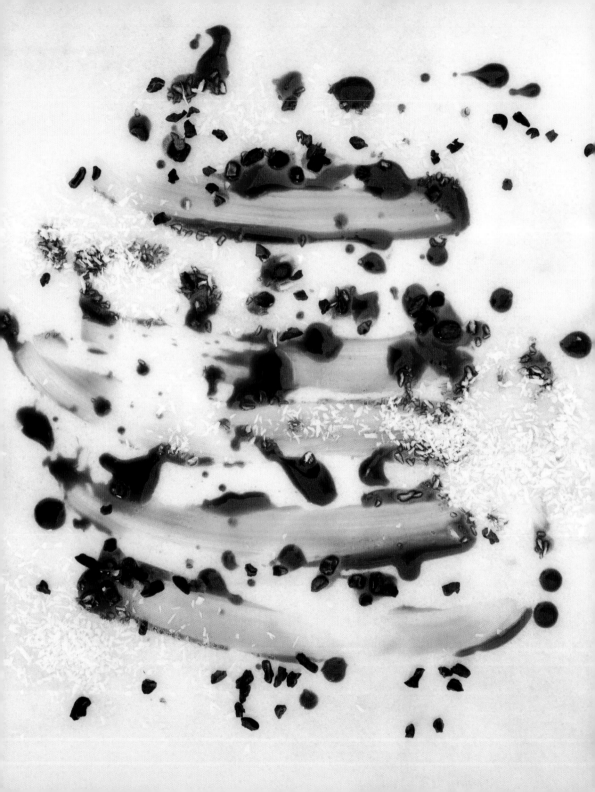

# Afternoon Tea

Everyone loves to indulge in a bit of something decadent! And afternoon tea on our retreats gives everyone a little treat. I usually offer something sweet and more often than not with chocolate in it as it's always a favourite!

I feel our love affair with chocolate is justified as it is such a beneficial food to eat. It's full of nutrients that make us feel happy, in love and blissful. Chocolate itself is a very bitter tasting food, which I personally enjoy and eat raw cacao (chocolate) nibs most days sprinkled on my breakfast. Although when using raw chocolate in these snacks I have sweetened it with agave nectar. You can use maple syrup or honey instead which alters the taste, making it more distinct.

All of the afternoon tea ideas are easy to make and keep really well either in the fridge or air tight containers so you can have something to hand when cravings for a naughty snack arise! These snacks are also great for taking with you to work or when travelling. Although I should point out that the chocolate will melt if it gets warm, so it's not as transportable as the shop bought chocolate. Therefore, it's best to keep your raw chocolate creations in the fridge.

I have also included some savoury ideas for those of us who crave salty snacks rather than sweet or you may just like variety!

# Nori Bites & Kale Chips

## Nori Bites

1 orange pepper
2 tsp ground cumin
200g cashews
100ml water
4 sushi nori sheets
1 tbsp sesame seeds

Blend the pepper, cumin, cashews and water in a blender until smooth to make the filling. Take a sheet of nori, place on a Paraflexx sheet, spoon half the cashew mixture on top and smooth fully over the sheet. Take another nori sheet, place on top and smooth out. Some of the filling mixture will come out of the sides but that's fine! Repeat the process with the other 2 nori sheets. Sprinkle sesame seeds over the top.

Dehydrate for 6 hours, then cut the nori sheets into snack size triangles. I find scissors work best for this. Continue to dehydrate overnight. The filling will have dried out and the nori bites crispy and delicious.

**Dehydration Time:** 18 hours
**Tip:** Vary the flavour of the filling by adding different spices such as chilli, coriander, curry powder or any herbs.

## Kale Chips

600g kale
100g cashews
100ml water
5 tsp wasabi powder
½ tsp salt

Roughly tear the kale leaves into large pieces, discarding the stalks as they are too woody to eat. Put the kale into a bowl. Add the cashews, water, wasabi powder and salt to a blender and blend until smooth.

Pour the cashew mixture over the kale and massage it into the kale with your hands ensuring all the kale is thoroughly coated.

Spread the coated kale onto a Paraflexx sheet in a thin even layer and dehydrate overnight.

**Dehydration Time:** Overnight
**Tip:** You can add any flavour you like to the cashew mixture e.g. tomato, olive, pepper, chilli...

# Trail Mix & Cucumber with Tapenade

## Trail Mix

250g tomatoes
1 small onion
1 clove garlic
2 tsp chilli flakes
2 tbsp olive oil
Pinch of salt and pepper
300g sunflower seeds
100g cacao nibs
250g pumpkin seeds
250g raisins
50g sprouted buckwheat

Add the tomatoes, onion, garlic, chilli flakes and olive oil to a food processor. Process for about a minute or until they've blended into a purée. Season with salt and pepper. Pour the mixture into a bowl and stir in the sunflower seeds so they are well coated. Put in to dehydrate overnight.

Once the tomato mixture has dried onto the sunflower seeds, break up into small pieces and put into a bowl. Mix in the remaining ingredients.

**Dehydration Time:** Overnight
**Tip:** The trail mix will keep for 4 weeks.

## Cucumber with Tapenade

1 cucumber
30g black dry pitted olives
100g capers

Slice the cucumber into rounds about 5mm thick. Place the cucumber slices onto kitchen paper to soak up the excess water.

Add the olives and the capers to a food processor and process for a minute or until the and capers are blended together. You will have a rough mixture so don't try and over process to make a smooth purée.

Place a teaspoonful of the tapenade mixture into the middle of each piece of cucumber.

The coolness of the fresh cucumber offsets the saltiness of the tapenade beautifully.

**Makes:** 20 pieces
**Tip:** You can decorate with small pieces of red pepper, sundried tomato or pine nuts.

# Raw Chocolates & Truffles

## Basic Raw Chocolate

> 200g cacao butter
> 50g cacao powder
> 30ml agave nectar

Cut the cacao butter into small pieces and place in a bowl. Melt the cacao butter either in a dehydrator or by using a bain marie. Once melted add in the cacao powder and agave syrup. Whisk together until glossy.

This is your basic raw chocolate mixture. Just use as is or you can add any variety of ingredients to flavour. Some suggestions are as follows:

## Salted Caramel

> 50ml basic raw chocolate mixture
> 1 tbsp rapeseed oil
> 1 tbsp coconut oil
> 1 tbsp honey
> 1 tbsp agave nectar
> 1 tsp vanilla extract
> ½ tsp salt

Mix the rapeseed oil, coconut oil, honey, agave nectar, vanilla extract and salt together. Pour into a chocolate mould, so the layer is about 2-3 mm thick, and put in the freezer to set. Take out when set and pour the basic raw chocolate mixture on top. Put back in the freezer to set.

## Orange & Ginger Chocolates

> 50ml basic raw chocolate mixture
> 3 drops orange essential oil
>   (food grade)
> ½ tbsp raw cacao powder
> 1 tsp ground ginger

Mix all the ingredients into the basic raw chocolate mixture. Pour into a chocolate mould and place in the freezer to set.

## Truffles

> 250g almonds
> 8 Medjool dates
> 1 tsp vanilla extract
> ½ tsp salt
> 15g cacao powder

Process the almonds in a food processor until they resemble chunky breadcrumbs. Add the pitted dates, vanilla extract and salt. Process until mixture sticks together.

Take a tablespoon size of the mixture and using your hands, shape into a ball. Shake the cacao powder out onto a plate and then roll the ball in the powder to coat it. Repeat until all the almond mixture is used up.

**Makes:** 18 truffles
**Tip:** You can roll the truffles in desiccated coconut instead of raw cacao powder.

# Flapjack & Raw Chocolate Brownies

## Flapjack

- 50ml rapeseed oil
- 30ml coconut oil
- 30ml honey
- 30ml agave nectar
- 1 tsp vanilla extract
- Pinch of salt
- 200g fine milled porridge oats
- 100g raisins

Add rapeseed oil, coconut oil, honey, agave nectar, vanilla extract and salt to a blender and blend for 30 seconds to make a smooth liquid which tastes like melted butter!

Put the porridge oats and raisins into a bowl and pour the "buttery" liquid in. Mix well.

Line a tray with baking paper and pour out the oat mixture. Dehydrate overnight and then put into the freezer.

**Freezing Time:** 2 hours
**Dehydration Time:** Overnight
**Makes:** 12 pieces
**Tip:** Add the honey and agave nectar to the measuring jug after the oil as it slides out of the jug more easily!

## Chocolate Brownies

- 75g walnuts
- 200g pecans
- 150g Medjool dates
  (weight with stone in)
- 50g cacao powder
- 1 tsp vanilla extract
- 2 tbsp desiccated coconut
- Pinch of salt

Add the walnuts to a food processor and pulse the nuts for a few seconds at a time to break them into small chunks. Empty into a bowl and set to one side.

Put the pecans into the food processor and process until they resemble breadcrumbs. Add the pitted dates, cacao powder, vanilla extract, desiccated coconut & salt and process for a couple of minutes until a sticky mixture (not crumbly) is formed.

Add this mixture to the walnuts and combine. Press the final mixture into a tin and refrigerate for an hour. Cut into pieces and serve.

**Makes:** 10 large or 20 small pieces
**Tip:** You can vary this by adding dried fruit such as raisins or cranberries.

# Lemon Cookies & Chocolate Bark

## Lemon Cookies

  250g cashews
  50g desiccated coconut
  50g lucuma powder
  2 lemons
  3 tbsp agave nectar

Add the cashews to a food processor and grind until they resemble fine bread crumbs. Add the desiccated coconut, lucuma powder, the rind of 1 lemon and the juice of both lemons plus agave nectar. Process for a couple of minutes until all ingredients stick together and form a dough like mixture.

With a teaspoon, spoon out a small piece of the "dough" onto a Paraflexx sheet. With a fork, press down onto the back of the mixture to form a cookie shape. The fork also leaves a nice imprint on the cookie. Repeat with the remaining mixture.

Dehydrate for approximately 7 hours to create a moist yet firm cookie.

**Dehydration Time:** 7 hours  **Makes:** 20
**Tip:** They go beautifully with the Lime Mousse in the Dessert section.

## Chocolate Bark

  200ml basic chocolate
    recipe (see pg 62)
  Pumpkin seeds
  White chia seeds
  Dried cranberries

Pour the melted chocolate mixture into a tray to make a layer approximately 3 mm thick. Then sprinkle seeds and cranberries over to make a pretty pattern.

Place in the freezer to set. I find that 2 hours is the optimal time for the bark to set.

Break into pieces and serve.

**Freezing Time:** 2 hours
**Tip:** You can sprinkle any crushed nuts or seeds on top.

# Dinner

Dinners are a special occasion although also an everyday meal. I like the contrast of making something sophisticated to eat that is full of flavours and textures yet has an elegance and ease to the creation of it.

All the recipes here have been put together in the way I serve dinner on our retreats, therefore, you will find a number of recipes within one dinner: the main dish plus sides. This gives you an idea of how to put a meal together and what goes with what. Of course, you don't have to create every dish provided in one dinner menu! You can pick what you fancy and just make that. You can also mix and match the recipes. For example you could use the parsnip rice, which is found in the satay dish, with the curry!

I want to mention that there are a few of these dishes that make use of a dehydrator which is not a common everyday kitchen utensil. If you don't have one, you can use an oven on a low setting.

I love the flavours of the dishes created in this section. I've thought about the cooked dishes I enjoy and their unique flavours to recreate a raw version. This is the basis of how you start to create your own dishes. What flavours do you enjoy and how can you adapt them into a raw version? Hopefully by starting to make some of my dishes you will be inspired to experiment. As I always say to people, make dishes to your tastes as when you do you're more likely to include raw food into your everyday diet.

The beauty of creating a raw food dinner menu is you can make so much ahead of time. There is no rushing because as I say to my guests, it can't burn!

Enjoy these dinners to feel amazing and radiant.

# Sunshine Stuffed Tomatoes with Garlic Oranges

## Sunshine Stuffed Tomatoes

2 beef tomatoes
1 small onion (quartered)
100g sunflower seeds
½ tbsp agave nectar
1 clove garlic
½ tsp cinnamon
½ tsp cayenne pepper
2 tsp smoked paprika
½ tbsp lucuma powder
1 tbsp olive oil
½ lemon
15g dill
1 corn on the cob
Salt and pepper

Slice the top end off the tomatoes (the end with the stalk!) and deseed the tomatoes. Rub the tomatoes with olive oil, salt and pepper. Dehydrate for 4 hours, although this is optional.

Add the chopped onion, sunflower seeds, agave nectar, cinnamon, cayenne pepper, smoked paprika and lucuma to a food processor.

Process for 1 minute to break up the sunflower seeds.

Add olive oil and enough water to make a pâté consistency. Process for a further minute.

Empty the mixture into a bowl and add in the juice from the lemon. Finely chop the dill and add to the mixture. Carefully cut the corn kernels off the cob and mix into the sunflower mixture. Season with salt and pepper.

Stuff the mixture into the tomatoes and replace the top of the tomato.

## Garlic Oranges

1 orange (peeled)
1 clove garlic
Splash of olive oil
Salt and pepper

Slice the orange into thin circles and place on a plate. Crush the garlic and sprinkle over the orange. Drizzle with olive oil and season with salt and pepper.

**Dehydration Time:** 4 hours (optional)
**Serves:** 2
**Tip:** Use a grapefruit spoon to easily scoop out the tomato seeds.

# Pizza with Coleslaw

## Pizza

250g buckwheat
  (soaked and sprouted)
150g sunflower seeds
50g sundried tomatoes in oil
2 tbsp olive oil
100ml water
1 tsp salt
3 tomatoes
½ onion
1 Medjool date

Put the buckwheat in a bowl, cover with water and leave overnight to soak. Drain the water and rinse the buckwheat. Leave the buckwheat for a further day to sprout. Rinse before using.

Add buckwheat to a food processor, along with the sunflower seeds, sun-dried tomatoes, olive oil, water and salt. Process to a thick "dough". Spread the "dough" out in a circle on a Paraflexx sheet to make your pizza base and dehydrate for 4 hours, flip and dehydrate overnight.

Add the tomatoes, onion and pitted date to the food processor, pulse to blend together. Spread the tomato sauce on the pizza base and dehydrate for a further 4 hours.

Top with your favourite toppings or choose from the following: tomato slices and basil; artichoke, spinach, pine nuts and capers; mushrooms marinated in tamari and olive oil.

## Coleslaw

250g white cabbage
150g carrot
2 tbsp rapeseed oil
1 tbsp apple cider vinegar
1 tsp Dijon mustard
Salt and pepper

Slice the cabbage finely and grate the carrot. Add both vegetables to a bowl.

In a separate bowl, mix the vinegar, oil and mustard together with a fork and season with salt and pepper. Pour over the cabbage and carrot and mix well.

**Sprouting Time:** 36 hours  **Dehydration Time:** 20 hours  **Serves:** 2
**Tip:** The pizza base can be made in advance and stored in the refrigerator for a few days.  The coleslaw will last well for a couple of days in the refrigerator too.

# Tomato Risotto with Fresh Green Salad

## Tomato Risotto

> 5 tomatoes
> Olive oil
> 300g cauliflower
> 25g pine nuts
> 150ml almond milk (see pg 26)
> Salt and pepper

Cut 3 tomatoes into quarters and place on a Paraflexx sheet, drizzle with olive oil and season with salt and pepper. Dehydrate for 8 hours. Or you can oven roast at 180°C for 45 minutes.

Add the cauliflower and pine nuts to a food processor. Process until the cauliflower resembles rice. Place into a bowl.

Pour the almond milk in a blender along with half the dehydrated tomatoes and 2 fresh tomatoes. Blend for 10 seconds.

Process the tomatoes until just blended into the almond milk so you can still see bits of tomato, as this adds texture.

Add the tomato almond milk mixture to the cauliflower and season with lots of salt and pepper.

## Fresh Green Salad

> 1 little gem lettuce
> 1 stick celery
> 50g cucumber
> 1 spring onion
> Herbs of your choice
> 1 lime

Tear the little gem lettuce into large pieces, chop the celery into chunks, slice the cucumber into semi-circles, cut the spring onion into small pieces and finely chop your choice of herbs. Squeeze lime juice over the salad and serve with the risotto.

**Dehydration Time:** 8 hours  **Serves:** 2
**Tip:** You can warm the risotto through by putting it in the dehydrator for an hour.

Notes

# Courgetti with Pesto with Tomato & Onion Salad

## Courgetti with Pesto

50g pine nuts
30g basil
1 tsp salt
4 tbsp olive oil
500g courgette

Put the pine nuts, basil, salt and olive oil into a food processor. Process until you have a thick sauce the consistency of pesto.

Spiralize the courgette to make the "courgetti". Place into a bowl and spoon 5 tablespoon of the pesto onto the courgetti. With your hands, massage the pesto into the courgette. Leave to marinate for 30 minutes.

To serve, pile the pesto courgetti into the middle of a plate and top with the tomato and onion salad.

## Tomato & Onion Salad

100g tomato
30g onion
½ tbsp balsamic vinegar
Salt and pepper

Slice the tomato and onion thinly, place in a bowl. Pour in the balsamic vinegar and season with salt and pepper. Leave to marinate for 30 minutes.

**Marinating Time:** 30 minutes - 1 hour  **Serves:** 2
**Tip:** This recipe makes more pesto than is needed. The remainder can be stored in the fridge. It's also good stuffed in marinated mushrooms.

Notes

# Beetroot Chilli with "Refried Beans", Pico de Gallo & Guacamole

## Beetroot Chilli

300g beetroot
100g tomato
50g onion
½ red jalapeño chilli pepper
3cm piece dried chipotle chilli
1 stick celery
½ tsp acai berry powder
½ tbsp maca powder
½ tbsp cacao powder
2 tsp ground coriander
1 tsp salt

Peel and grate the beetroot. Add to a bowl and place to one side whilst you prepare the sauce.

Add the remaining ingredients to a food processor and process until you have a chunky sauce. Make sure the dried chipotle chilli has been blended into the sauce. Stir the tomato chilli sauce into the beetroot and leave to marinate for an hour or longer.

## Guacamole

1 avocado
Tabasco to taste
½ lemon

Mash the avocado with a fork to create a chunky texture. Stir in the Tabasco and juice from the lemon. Best eaten fresh.

## Pico de Gallo

200g tomato
50g white onion
15g fresh coriander
½ green chilli
½ lime
Salt and pepper

Chop the tomatoes and onions into cubes and finely chop the coriander and chilli. Add all the ingredients to a bowl. Juice the lime and pour over the fresh ingredients. Season with salt and pepper.

## "Refried Beans"

200g sunflower seeds
6 sundried tomatoes in oil
2 tsp ground cumin
2 tsp salt
1 tbsp rapeseed oil

Add all the ingredients to a food processor and mix together for 2 minutes. You want the mixture to clump together slightly. Crumble the mixture onto a Paraflexx sheet and dehydrate for 8 hours.

**To Serve:** In a cooks ring, half fill with refried bean mixture. Fill to the top with the beetroot chilli mixture. Finish with a spoon of guacamole on the top and pico de gallo around the outside. **Note:** If you wish to eat this with meat try it with steak strips – fry the steak strips up and serve on top of the beetroot chilli. **Serves:** 2

# Tabbouleh Stuffed Peppers with Falafel & Garlic Green Beans

## Tabbouleh Stuffed Peppers Peppers

2 long red pointed peppers
100g tomatoes
75g artichokes in oil
15g mint
15g parsley
½ lemon
Salt and pepper

Carefully cut the red peppers in half and scoop out the seeds. Optionally, you can dehydrate the pepper for 7 hours, which will give them a more roasted appearance. You can of course oven roast the peppers!

Finely chop tomatoes, artichoke and herbs and put into a bowl. Juice the lemon and add to the fresh ingredients. Season with salt and pepper. Set aside to marinate for 30 minutes. To serve, stuff the tabbouleh into the pepper. **Serves:** 2
**Dehydration Time:** 7 hours (optional)

## Falafel

150g pumpkin seeds
1 tbsp tahini
1 tsp cayenne pepper
2 tsp ground cumin
2 tbsp olive oil
2 cloves garlic
½ lemon
Large pinch of salt
50ml water

Process the pumpkin seeds in a food processor to resemble fine crumbs. Add tahini, cayenne pepper, cumin and olive oil. Juice the lemon and add to the mixture. Peel the garlic and add. Process together for a minute or until the mixture starts to stick together. Then add the water and process for a further 30 seconds.

Using your hands, take a small amount of the mixture and shape into a ball. Repeat with the remaining mixture. Dehydrate for 6 hours, so the outside is crisp and the inside still slightly moist. If you don't have a dehydrator you can put them in a low oven for 45 minutes.
**Dehydration Time:** 6 hours **Makes:** 12 balls

## Garlic Green Beans

100g green beans
1 large clove of garlic
½ tbsp olive oil
½ lemon
Big pinch of salt

Top and tail the green beans and place in a dish. Peel and crush the garlic and sprinkle over the green beans.

Juice lemon and mix into oil with a big pinch of salt. Toss the green beans and garlic in this mixture and dehydrate for 6 hours. Or alternatively pan fry for 5 minutes.
**Dehydration Time:** 6 hours **Serves:** 2

# "Roast" Vegetable Satay with Parsnip Rice

## "Roast" Vegetables

200g courgette
300g aubergine
1 orange pepper
4 mushrooms
4 tbsp rapeseed oil
2 tbsp balsamic vinegar
½ tbsp agave nectar
1 tsp ground ginger
Small pinch of salt

Chop the courgette into circles 1 cm thick. Cut the aubergine into 1 cm thick cubes. Cut the pepper into large pieces and cut the mushrooms in half. Place all the vegetables into a large bowl.

Mix together rapeseed oil, balsamic vinegar, agave nectar and ground ginger and season with salt.

Pour mixture over the vegetable and toss well to coat them all. Marinate for an hour.

Alternate the vegetables onto wooden skewers and dehydrate for 6 hours or if you don't have a dehydrator, place in the oven at 180°C for 45 minutes

## Satay Sauce

100g walnuts
½ lemon
1 tbsp tamari
3 tbsp coconut milk
1cm cube of fresh ginger
50g white onion
1 tsp chilli flakes
1 tsp coriander seeds
½ tsp agave nectar

Place all the ingredients into a food processor and process until they have mixed together. You will find you have a slightly chunky texture with the nuts and onion, this is fine. Place in the dehydrator with the vegetable skewers to warm or use a sauce pan.

## Parsnip Rice

200g parsnip
50 ml coconut milk
30g macadamia nuts
1 tsp salt

Peel the parsnips and cut into large chunks. Add the parsnip chunks to a food processor along with the coconut milk, nuts and salt. Process until the parsnip is finely chopped and resembles rice.

**Marinating Time:** 1 hour  **Dehydration Time:** 6 hours  **Serves:** 2
**Tip:** You can substitute the vegetables for any other ones you wish or even use prawns or chicken which are cooked of course!

# Almond "Meatballs" in Tomato Sauce & Courgette Tagliatelli

## Almond "Meatballs"

125g almonds
1 stick celery
1 apple
2 sundried tomatoes in oil
1 tbsp tamari
1 tsp smoked paprika
1 tsp garlic granules

Add almonds to a food processor and process until the nuts are broken down into small pieces. Cut the apple into quarters and the celery into 3 pieces and add to the food processor along with the sundried tomatoes and smoked paprika and garlic granules. Process for a minute or until all the ingredients are mixed together.

Take a large teaspoon of the mixture and form into a ball. Place the balls onto a Paraflexx sheet and dehydrate overnight.

## Tomato Sauce

250g tomaotes
2 sundried tomatoes in oil
1 clove garlic
Salt and pepper

Quarter the tomatoes and add to a food processor with the sundried tomatoes and garlic. Process until you have a chunky sauce. Season with salt and pepper.

## Courgette Tagliatelli

350g courgette

With a vegetable peeler, peel off the green skin of the courgette and discard. Still using the vegetable peeler, peel off strips from the courgette to form the pasta tagliatelle shape.

**To Serve:** Put a half the courgette tagliatelle in the middle of a plate, cover with the tomato sauce then place 3 almond balls per person on top. For a quick meal, forgo the meatballs. **Dehydration Time:** Overnight **Makes:** 6 meatballs **Serves:** 2

Notes

# Cauliflower Madras with Onion Bhajis & Mango Tamarind Salsa

## Cauliflower Madras

- 200g tomatoes
- 50g white onion
- 1 clove garlic
- 1 Medjool date
- 4 cardamom pods
- 2 tbsp madras curry powder
- 50ml almond milk (see page 26)
- 400g cauliflower

Chop tomatoes into quarters and add to a food processor along with onion, garlic and pitted date. Process for 2 minutes or until ingredients have blended together. Remove seeds from the cardamom pods and crush in a pestle and mortar then add to the tomato mixture with the curry powder and almond milk. Pulse briefly to combine. Chop the cauliflower into small pieces and place in a bowl. Pour the sauce over and stir to coat the cauliflower. Warm and serve.

## Mango Tamarind Salsa

- 200g carrots
- 1 tbsp desiccated coconut
- 2 tsp tamarind concentrate
- 50ml water
- ½ mango
- 30g fresh coriander

Grate carrots and place in a bowl. Add in coconut. Finely chop the mango and fresh coriander then add to carrot and coconut. Mix the tamarind with the water to make a runny paste, stir into the fresh ingredients. Leave to marinate for 30 minutes.

## Onion Bhajis

- 50ml rapeseed oil
- 50ml water
- 150g sunflower seeds
- 100g carrots
- 2 tsp chilli flakes
- 2 tsp ground coriander
- 2 tsp ground cumin
- 1 tsp turmeric
- 1 tbsp red wine vinegar
- 1 tsp lemon juice
- 1 tsp salt
- 3 tsp cumin seeds
- 3 tsp coriander seeds
- 250g white onion

Add the rapeseed oil and water to a blender, then add the sunflower seeds. Chop the carrots into large pieces then add to the blender along with 1 teaspoon of the chilli flakes, ground coriander, ground cumin, turmeric, red wine vinegar and lemon juice. Blend until a smooth batter is formed. Spoon the bhaji batter into a bowl. Stir in the remaining 1 teaspoon of chilli flakes, coriander seeds and cumin seeds.

Slice the onion into thin strips and stir into the batter so the onion is well coated. Spoon out 1 tablespoon of onion bhaji mixture onto a Paraflexx tray, repeat with remaining mixture and dehydrate overnight.

**Dehydration Time:** Overnight **Serves:** 2
**Tip:** You can replace the cauliflower with mushrooms for a mushroom curry.

# Christmas Dinner: Mushroom Nut Loaf, Spiced Red Cabbage, Cranberry Sauce, Parsnip Mash, Brussels Sprouts & Chestnuts, Carrot & Orange Ribbons with Black Ginger Fizz

## Mushroom Nut Loaf

125g Brazil nuts
200g mushrooms
3 spring onions
½ apple
2 dried figs
1 tsp smoked paprika
2 tsp ground coriander
1 tsp smoked salt
1 tbsp rapeseed oil
½ tbsp rice mirin
½ tbsp plum seasoning

Add the nuts to a food processor and process until the nuts resemble breadcrumbs. Remove from the food processor and add to a bowl.

Add mushrooms to the food processor, there's no need to wash it! Process the mushrooms until they become a purée, you may have to do half the mushrooms at a time. Add the mushroom purée to the nuts along with the remaining ingredients and mix well.

Spoon into small individual loaf tins (I use silicone hearts). Dehydrate overnight. The next morning, remove loaves from tins and dehydrate for a further 6 hours.

**Dehydration Time:** 18 hours
**Serves:** 2
**Storage:** Loaves store up to 2 days in the refrigerator in an airtight container

Notes

## Spiced Red Cabbage

1 pink lady apple
250g red cabbage
100g white onion
2 Medjool dates
50ml red wine vinegar
100ml water
½ tsp cinnamon
½ tsp nutmeg
10 cloves (heads only)
3 cloves garlic
½ tsp salt

Chop the apple into small cubes, cut the onion into thin slices and shred the cabbage into strips. Put all the vegetables into a bowl.

Add the remaining ingredients to a blender and blend for a 10 seconds or until the dates have blended into the water and vinegar to make a dressing.

Pour the dressing over the vegetables and marinate for an hour or even overnight.

**Marinating Time:** 1 hour – overnight

## Cranberry Sauce

25g dried cranberries
100g frozen cherries
½ tbsp agave nectar
15ml water

Soak the cranberries for 30 minutes in water, drain and put the cranberries into a blender along with the frozen cherries, water and agave nectar.

Blend for 10 seconds to form a sauce with texture.

**Soaking Time:** 30 minutes

## Parsnip Mash

300g parsnip
5 tbsp rapeseed oil
¼ tsp grated nutmeg
½ tsp salt

Peel the parsnips, cut into large chunks and put in a food processor. Add the nutmeg and season with salt. Process the parsnip until it's finely chopped. Then slowly add the rapeseed oil allowing it to blend the parsnip together to resemble mash.

**Preparation Time:** 10 minutes

## Carrot & Orange Ribbons

200g carrots
½ orange
1 tsp runny honey
Salt

Peel the carrots and discard the peel. Then using the vegetable peeler, peel the carrot length ways to form ribbons. Put into a bowl. Juice the orange and mix with the honey and season with salt. Toss the carrots with the orange dressing and leave to marinate for 1 hour. This allows the carrots to soften.

**Marinating Time:** 1 hour

## Brussels Sprouts & Chestnuts

100g Brussels sprouts
50g cooked chestnuts
1 tsp mustard seeds
½ lemon
Salt

Peel the Brussels sprouts and quarter. Add to a bowl, chop the chestnuts into quarters and add to Brussels sprouts. Toss the sprouts and chestnuts in the mustard seeds, the rind of the lemon and season with salt.

**Preparation Time:** 15 minutes

## Black Ginger Fizz

200g black grapes
1cm cubed fresh ginger
½ lime
500ml sparkling water

Blend the grapes, ginger, lime and 100 ml of sparking water. Strain through a nut milk bag to remove the grape skin as they don't blend well. Once strained add remaining sparkling water and serve.

**Preparation Time:** 10 minutes

......................................................

**Notes:**

# Mushroom Stroganoff on Spring Greens

250g chestnut mushrooms
250g Forestiere mushrooms
1 tbsp paprika
4 tbsp olive oil
1 tbsp tamari
2 Medjool dates
100ml water

100g onion
150 ml cashew yoghurt
  (see pg 18)
1 tsp salt
Handful of parsley
200g spring greens

Cut both the chestnut and Forestiere mushrooms into slices and rub in paprika. Mix the oil and tamari together and pour over the mushrooms. Use your hands to ensure mushrooms are thoroughly coated in the oil and tamari. Marinate for 1 hour. Then place the marinated mushrooms on a Paraflexx sheet and dehydrate for 4 hours.

Add the pitted dates, salt and water to a blender and blend until a runny paste forms. Cut the onions into thin slices and add to the date paste. Spread on a Paraflexx sheet, pouring out all the date paste too. Be careful not to spill the date paste off the sides of the dehydrator tray as it is runny! Dehydrate for 5 hours.

Place the dehydrated mushrooms and onions with all the dried date paste into a bowl. Pour over the cashew yoghurt and mix thoroughly. Put the bowl into the dehydrator for an hour.

Cut the spring greens into thin strips, place in a bowl and pour boiling water over them. Leave for 10 seconds to blanch. Drain the water and rinse in cold water, shaking off any excess.

Serve the mushroom stroganoff on top of the blanched spring greens.

**Dehydration Time:** 6 hours  **Serves:** 2
**Tip:** This may seem a long procedure with the dehydrating but it's worth it and it's just about planning the timing. It's a very rich dish.

# Butternut Squash "Spaghetti" with Lemon & Tarragon Dressing

30g cashews
50g macadamia nuts
30g tarragon
Handful of dill
1 lemon

1 tbsp olive oil
100ml water
Salt and pepper
450g butternut squash

Add the cashew and macadamia nuts to a food processor. Strip the tarragon leaves off the woody stalk and discard the stalk. Add the leaves to the food processor. Peel the rind off the lemon and add to the food processor along with the dill, juice of the lemon, olive oil and water. Season with salt and pepper. Process the ingredients until you have a smooth sauce.

Chop off the end of the butternut squash and use the end without seeds. Peel the butternut squash and cut into quarters. With a spirilizer make the butternut squash into spaghetti.

Put the butternut squash spaghetti into a bowl with the sauce and toss together.

**Preparation Time:** 30 minutes **Serves:** 2
**Tip:** Serve with lemon olives, chopped red pepper on a bed of fresh green leaves.

Notes

# Dessert

Desserts are a double-edged part of the meal for me. My ladies on our retreats usually love desserts yet I personally don't have a sweet tooth! However, I've overcome that and made some simple and delicious dessert dishes that satisfy the desire to complete a meal with something sweet.

Of course, you can make the dish more or less sweet by adjusting the quantity of sweetener specified in a recipe.

I do feel we shouldn't eat too much sugar yet this book is not here to tell you what you should or should not be eating. I want you to feel good. Rules about what you should eat can take away the pleasure of eating. It imposes the question "Can I eat this?" which creates anxiety about whether you can truly enjoy what is placed in front of you. With that in mind, eat dessert and see how it makes you feel.

The range of desserts in this section vary from light sorbet to heavy cheesecake. It's difficult to eat a lot of the cheesecake, so a small piece really will fill you up. It will make you feel good that you've eaten something delicious without leaving you stuffed and uncomfortable.

There is also a taste of the exotic with the rose infused cardamom and rhubarb pots and the big kid in you will love the banana split. Enjoy making and eating them. Lastly, raw desserts are a great way to introduce other people to the concept of eating raw food, for these desserts are not what people expect raw food to be.

# Berry Sorbet

250g frozen mixed berries
1 tbsp agave nectar (optional)
1/2 tsp vanilla extract
50ml water

This recipe really is simplicity itself as all you have to do is add all the ingredients to a high powered blender! The water is necessary to ensure the blade will go around.

The agave nectar is optional as it depends on your sweet tooth since frozen berries can be tart.

Blend for 20-30 seconds. You have now formed the sorbet. Serve in pretty bowls either on its own or decorated with other fruits such as fresh berries, figs or even chopped nuts.

You can substitute the frozen berries for any other fruit you like such as mango, cherry or pineapple. Play around to create different flavoured sorbets.

**Preparation Time:** 5 minutes  **Serves:** 2
**Tip:** You can use any leftover sorbet to pour into ice lolly moulds to form ice lollies. When you freeze the sorbet it becomes very hard.

Notes

# Lemon & Raspberry Cheesecake

150g almonds
150g Medjool dates
1 tsp vanilla extract
250g cashews
3 lemons

3 tbsp coconut oil
3 tbsp agave nectar
100ml water
225g raspberries

Add the almonds, pitted dates and vanilla extract to a food processor. Process until the almonds resemble bread crumbs and the mixture sticks together when you press it in your hands. Empty the almond mixture into a 20 cm diameter silicone cake dish. Press the almond mixture into the dish and use your fingers making sure it sticks together. This is your cheesecake base.

Add the cashews to a blender along with the zest and juice of the lemons, coconut oil and agave nectar. Blend together. This will be a very thick mixture. It's best to blend before adding the water so you

can slowly add the water a bit at a time to get the consistency of cream cheese. You may not need all 100 ml of water if you have very juicy lemons.

Spoon the cashew lemon mixture onto the top of the almond base. Smooth out and place the cheesecake into the freezer to set. It also makes it easier to remove the cheesecake from the mould when it is frozen! Remove the cheesecake from the freezer 1 hour before serving to thaw.

In a bowl, mash the raspberries with a fork and spoon them over the top of the cheesecake.

**Freezing Time:** 2 hours  **Storage:** Keep in the freezer for up to 1 month  **Serves:** 8
**Tip:** You can create any variety of flavours of cheesecake by replacing the lemon with your choice of ingredients. For example cacao powder, mint extract or any fruit.

Notes

# Coconut, Orange, Passion Fruit & Banana Gelato

700g frozen bananas
2 passion fruit
150ml coconut milk

2 tsp orange essential oil
 (food grade)
25g goji berries

Add all the ingredients to a high powered blender such as a Vitamix. Blend for approximately 30 seconds to form a gelato, a soft ice cream.

Serve immediately and freeze any leftovers.

This is a very easy way to make gelato, which is loved by children and adults alike. The base of the gelato is frozen bananas and a liquid such as coconut milk, almond milk, water or cream.

You can vary the flavours to make all sorts of gelato. Try adding in fruits such as cherry, raspberry, strawberry or mango. Add cacao powder to make chocolate gelato and vary it by adding in mint for mint chocolate, or orange for orange chocolate or cacao nibs for chocolate chip gelato. Have fun experimenting with your favourite flavours!

**Preparation Time:** 5 minutes  **Serves:** 2 very large portions
**Tip:** Make sure to peel and chop up the bananas before freezing.

Notes

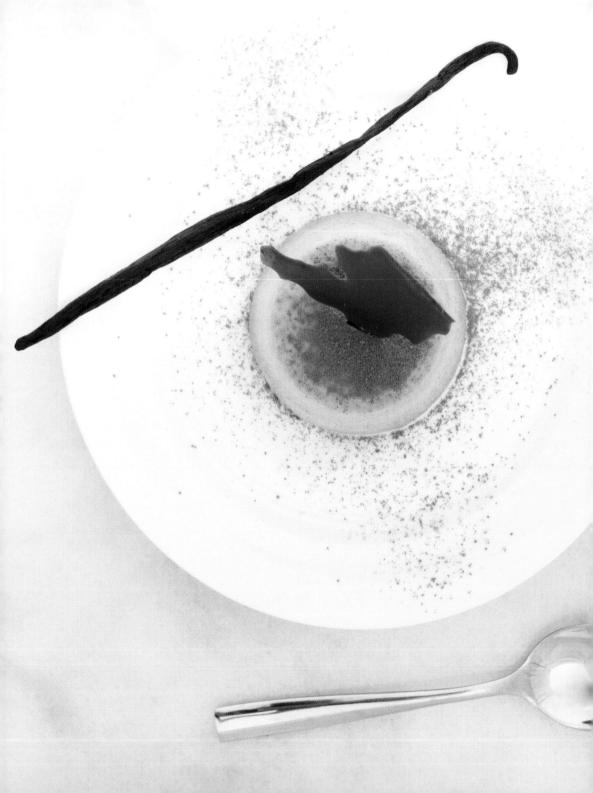

# Banana Crème

250g peeled bananas
½ lemon
1 tbsp coconut oil

1 tbsp agave nectar
1 tbsp lucuma powder
1 tbsp tahini

This simple dessert is always a favourite and is very quick and easy to make.

Chop the bananas into pieces and add to a high speed blender. Add the juice of the lemon to the blender along with the remaining ingredients. Blend for 1 to 2 minutes or until the ingredients are thoroughly blended. You may find that you have to stop half way through and push the ingredients down towards the blades.

Pour the mixture into a muffin tray and freeze for at least 1 hour.

Remove from the freezer 30 minutes before serving and decorate with raw cacao powder using a sieve to sprinkle it over the top. It will resemble crème caramel!

**Preparation Time:** 5 minutes **Freezing Time:** 1 hour **Serves:** 4
**Tip:** You can make these a few days ahead of time. They store well in the freezer.

Notes

# Rose Infused Cardamom & Rhubarb Pots

15g white chia seeds
100ml almond milk
   (see pg 26)
3 cardamom pods
10g pistachios

Few drops of rose water
75g rhubarb (from a tin with
   syrup...yes not raw!)

Soak the chia seeds in 50 ml of almond milk. The chia seeds will absorb all the almond milk. When they have, add the remaining 50 ml of almond milk. You want it to be a thick pudding like consistency reminiscent of rice pudding.

Take the seeds out of the cardamom pods – a very important part! Crush them with a pestle and mortar to as fine a powder as you can. Stir this powder through the chia pudding mixture.

In the same pestle and mortar, without washing it, add the pistachios and crush them into small pieces. Set a few pieces to one side and stir the rest into the chia mixture. Stir in a few drops of rose water. Be careful not to overdo the rose water as it can be strong.

To serve put the chia pudding mixture into a pretty bowls and spoon rhubarb on top. Decorate with the remaining crushed pistachio nuts.

**Preparation Time:** 10 minutes  **Soaking Time:** 30 minutes  **Serves:** 2
**Tip:**  You can use fresh rhubarb stalks if you prefer. Pulse it in a food processor with some agave nectar to taste.  And yes, you can eat rhubarb stalks raw (it's a question I often get asked when I serve raw rhubarb... it's the leaves you can't eat).

Notes

# Lime Mousse

2 avocados
3 limes
2 tbsp coconut oil

2 tbsp agave nectar
1 tsp vanilla extract

Peel the avocado and cut into quarters, add to a food processor. Zest the limes and add to the avocado. Then juice the limes and add to the food processor along with the remaining ingredients.

Mix together for a couple of minutes until you have formed a smooth purée. You could use a blender instead if you wish. Make sure that the avocado is fully mixed in and there are no lumps.

Note you don't have to melt the coconut oil before adding to the food processor as the heat from the blades will ensure the coconut oil blends in thoroughly.

Spoon the lime mousse into 2 small dishes and refrigerate for at least 30 minutes before serving.

**Refrigerating Time:** 30 minutes - overnight  **Serves:** 3
**Tip:** Great with fresh fruit like figs. Try pairing with the Lemon Cookies on page 66 for something a bit richer.

Notes

# Spiced Chocolate Orange Ganache

2 avocados
1 orange
40g raw cacao butter melted
30g raw cacao powder
1 tbsp maca powder

1 tsp cinnamon
2 cloves
¼ tsp cayenne pepper powder
2 tbsp agave nectar

Ganache is a rich chocolate and cream affair which is replicated in this recipe with raw chocolate and avocado.

Place the flesh of the avocados into a food processor. Add the rind of the orange then its juice and mix with the avocado for 1 minute.

Add raw cacao powder, maca powder, spices and agave nectar to the mix. Blend together for 2 minutes until the ingredients have thoroughly mixed together. Scrape the sides down as needed.

Finally add in the melted raw cacao butter. To melt, cut the solid raw cacao butter into small pieces and add to a bain marie. Blend into the avocado mixture which will turn it glossy.

Spoon into a silicone cake mould and put into the freezer to set. Remove from the freezer 30 minutes before serving.

**Preparation Time:** 10 minutes  **Freezing Time:** 2 hours  **Serves:** 4
**Tip:** This is a bitter 'grown up' dessert but you can make it sweeter by adding more agave syrup or cutting down the cacao powder.

Notes

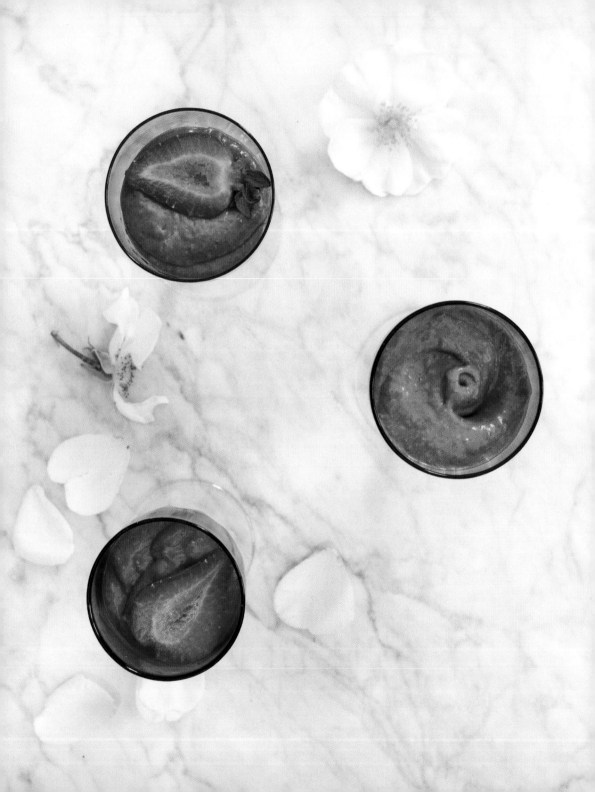

# Strawberry Chocolate Mousse

2 avocados
400g strawberries
2 tbsp cacao powder
2 tbsp coconut oil

60ml almond milk
    (optional, pg 26)
2 tbsp agave nectar
1 tsp vanilla extract

Place the flesh of the avocados into a food processor. Hull the strawberries and add to the food processor along with the remaining ingredients.

Blend together for a couple of minutes until you have formed a smooth purée. You could use a blender instead if you wish. Make sure all the avocado is fully mixed in and there are no lumps.

Note you do not have to melt the coconut oil before adding to the food processor as the heat from the blades will ensure the coconut oil blends in thoroughly.

Spoon the strawberry chocolate mousse into 2 beautiful serving glasses and refrigerate for an hour or until needed.

**Preparation Time:** 15 minutes  **Refrigerating Time:** 1 hour  **Serves:** 4
**Tip:** If you don't have raw cacao powder you can use a good quality cocoa powder.

Notes

# Apple Crumble

2 apples
¼ lemon
½ tbsp agave nectar

50g buckwheaties
(see pg 132)
3 dried figs

Quarter and core the apples and put into a food processor. Pulse until the apples are slightly broken down but have not turned into a purée. Add the juice from the lemon and the agave syrup and quickly pulse into the apples. You can omit or reduce the agave, especially if you have very sweet apples. The lemon juice is there just to help preserve some of the colour so the apples don't turn too brown.

Put the apple mixture into the bottom of a dish.

Without washing the food processor, add the buckwheaties and figs. Pulse until the figs are chopped up finely, you want a sticky mixture by combining these 2 ingredients together but still some texture from the buckwheaties. You will still have whole bits of buckwheat in this mixture, which is great as this is your crumble topping. Scatter the crumble topping on top of the apple and dehydrate for 6 hours. Serve with almond milk or for a non-vegan version you can use cream.

**Preparation Time:** 15 minutes **Dehydration Time:** 6 hours max **Serves:** 2
**Tip:** You can vary the fruit that you add to your crumble – try pear and blackberry, apricot, nectarine, cherry or gooseberry.

Notes

# Superfood Banana Split

## Ice Creams

 2 tsp psyllium husks
 ½ tsp cacao nibs
 2 tsp agave nectar
 1 tbsp water
 200g frozen banana
 50ml almond milk (see pg 26)
 1 tbsp lucuma powder
 1 tsp matcha tea powder
 1 tbsp dried mulberries

In a bowl add the psyllium husks, cacao nibs, agave nectar and water. Mix together to form a spongy mixture. This is your cookie dough. Form the "cookie dough" into small balls and put to one side.

Add the banana and almond milk to a blender and blend until smooth. Split the banana ice cream into 2 bowls. Into one bowl mix in the cookie dough balls and lucuma powder. Into the other bowl mix in the matcha tea powder and dried mulberries. Form the ice cream into balls and put into the freezer to harden whilst you continue with the sauces for the banana split.

## Sauces

 75g cashews
 75ml water
 1 tsp vanilla extract
 ½ tbsp agave nectar
 50g raspberries
 50ml water
 Basic raw chocolate (see pg 62)

Put the cashews, water, vanilla extract and agave nectar into a blender and blend until smooth. Empty out of the blender and put to one side. This is the vanilla cream sauce.

To make the raspberry cream sauce, without washing the blender, add the raspberries and water and blend until smooth. The remains of the cashews will blend in with the raspberries to create a beautiful pink sauce. If you wish to be very fancy you can sieve the raspberry cream sauce to remove any seeds left behind but this is optional.

Melt the raw chocolate and keep it warm so it doesn't set.

**To Serve:** You will need the following: 1 large banana, "cookie dough" lucuma ice cream, matcha tea ice cream, vanilla cream sauce, raspberry cream sauce, chocolate sauce and one fresh cherry. Cut the banana in half lengthways and lay along a dish. Place the ice cream balls in between the banana halves. Top the cookie dough lucuma ice cream with the raspberry cream sauce and top the matcha tea ice cream with the vanilla cream sauce. Drizzle the raw chocolate sauce over the top. Top with a cherry and serve with 2 spoons. **Note:** You will have more sauce than you need for this recipe but you can keep them in the fridge and use over fruit or more ice cream! **Serves:** 2
**Tip:** This makes a spectacular piece for a romantic dinner but make sure you drink lots of water after eating this as it contains psyllium husks.

# Juices & Smoothies

I love juices and smoothies. I eat a lot of them because they make me feel radiant, happy and full of energy. They are my go-to staple when I need a pick me up and I will let you in on a secret, they really help fuel me to lead my retreats with so much enthusiasm. So if you're not regularly consuming juices and smoothies, I do hope this section inspires you to start making some.

There are only 10 recipes in this section but in reality I could have put in 100! There are so many variations. When we run a smoothie workshop where guests make their own signature smoothie, every one is different which always highlights the endless possibilities of smoothie making.

I do believe all smoothies should be green! Of course, you miss out on all the pretty colours when you make only green ones yet for me the power of the smoothie is the green within it and I want that! The pictures we have taken were shot before the green ingredient was added to show you the variety of colour but if you check the recipe you will see the green vegetables included.

And I do believe juices should be mainly vegetable based and not fruit based! Fruit based juices to me just deliver too much sugar, so I concentrate on vegetable based ones. People often ask what is the difference between a juice and a smoothie, a juice has the fibre removed, it makes it easier to digest so the nutrients are absorbed into the body more quickly. A smoothie on the other hand takes longer to digest as it still has the fibre in it. With that in mind, I love a smoothie in the morning at breakfast time to help energise me for the day and a juice late afternoon to perk me up.

# Up-Beet Juice

½ red pepper
250g beetroot (fresh)
1 lime
½ cucumber

Deseed the red pepper and cut the leaves off the beetroot.

Cut the vegetables to a size that can fit into the funnel of your juicer.

Put the red pepper in first, followed by the beetroot, the lime (which doesn't need to be peeled) and lastly the cucumber.

Drink fresh.

**Makes:** 400 ml of juice
**Tip:** Red peppers are also called bell peppers or capsicums depending on your country. If you scrub the beetroot you don't need to peel it.

# Spiced Pear Juice

200g parsnips
2 sticks celery
150g fennel
1 pear
Nutmeg

Cut the vegetables to a size that can fit into the funnel of your juicer.

Put the parsnip in first, followed by the celery, fennel and finally the pear.

Grate the nutmeg on top of the juice and enjoy!

**Makes:** 250 ml of juice
**Tip:** If you scrub the parsnips you don't need to peel them.

Notes

# Orange Zing Juice

300g carrot
1 orange
200g sweet potato
10g ginger

Peel the orange and cut to size for your juicer.

Cut the vegetables to a size that can fit into the funnel of your juicer.

Put the carrots in, followed by the sweet potato, the ginger and finally the orange.

Enjoy!

**Makes:** 400 ml of juice
**Tip:** If you scrub the sweet potato you don't need to peel it.

# Beautiful Glow Juice

2 sticks celery
Handful parsley
1 lemon
½ cucumber

Cut the vegetables to a size that can fit into the funnel of your juicer.

Put the celery in, followed by the parsley, the lemon and finally the cucumber.

Drink straight away.

**Makes:** 400 ml of juice
**Tip:** This smoothie is great if you feel a cold coming on as it has loads of Vitamin C!

....................................................................

Notes

# Tropical Smoothie

½ mango
1 banana frozen
½ cm cubed fresh ginger
Large handful spinach
200ml water

Peel the mango and cut the fruit off the stone.

Place the mango fruit in your blender along with the frozen banana, ginger, spinach and water. Blend until smooth.

Serve and enjoy!

**Makes:** 300 ml of smoothie
**Tip:** Peel and slice the banana before freezing it.

# Creamy St. Clements Smoothie

2 oranges
1 lemon
½ avocado
½ mango
Large handful spinach
150ml water

Peel the oranges and lemon and cut into large chunks.

Peel the avocado and mango, remove the stones and cut into large chunks.

Place all the ingredients in a blender with the spinach and water. Blend until smooth.

**Makes:** 400 ml of juice
**Tip:** Good for your skin. You don't need to peel the lemon before juicing if you use unwaxed lemons.

Notes

# Fruity Strawberry Smoothie

200g strawberries
1 pear
1 nectarine
100g little gem lettuce
150ml water

Hull the strawberries. Cut the pear into large chunks and remove and discard the core. Remove the stone from the nectarine and discard. Chop the lettuce into chunks.

Add all the ingredients to the blender.

Blend until smooth.

**Makes:** 750 ml of smoothie
**Tip:** Out of season, frozen strawberries work great. They make the smoothie nice and cool.

# Herby Pineapple Smoothie

1 lime
300g pineapple
50ml coconut milk (tinned)
10 basil leaves
Small spring of rosemary
   (about 6 needles)
150ml water

Remove the skin from the pineapple and discard.

Cut the lime in half (you can use it unpeeled) and add to a blender. Cut the pineapple flesh into chunks and add to the blender along with the coconut milk, basil leaves, rosemary and water.

Blend until smooth. Drink immediately.

**Makes:** 500 ml of smoothie
**Tip:** To make variations on this smoothie, try different herbs.

........................................................................

Notes

# Refreshing Watermelon Smoothie

50g blackcurrants
500g watermelon
50g cherries
Big handful of fresh mint

Cut the skin off the watermelon and discard. Remove pips and discard. Cut the remaining watermelon up into large chunks.

Remove stones from the cherries and discard.

Add all ingredients to a blender and blend until smooth. Note this smoothie does not need water as there is a lot of water in the watermelon.

**Makes:** 600 ml of smoothie
**Tip:** You can buy frozen cherries with the pits already removed.

# Green Crusader Smoothie

100g blueberries
1 plum
1 apple
½ cucumber
50g kale
2 tsp Spirulina
250ml water

Remove the stone from the plum and discard. Cut the apple into large chunks and discard the core. Cut the cucumber into large chunks.

Add all ingredients to the blender and blend until smooth.

**Makes:** 750 ml of smoothie
**Tip:** You can add Spirulina to taste. Add more as you get more acclimatised to it.

Notes

# Equipment

### blender

A blender is a great way to make smoothies and mix things like sorbets and gelatos.

At Split Farthing Hall, we use a Vitamix. This is a top-end, very powerful blender that is easy to use. It quickly blends, purées and mixes. If you're going to be doing a lot of blending, a Vitamix is a great investment.

### dehydrator

Dehydrators slowly dry food by blowing dry air over it at a low temperature. They are ideal for creating "roasted", "cooked" or "baked" textures such as for the Lemon Cookies. Raw food is generally dehydrated at 42°C maximum.

Dehydrators come with mesh sheets, so for wet mixtures these need to be lined with non-stick liner sheets. At Split Farthing Hall, we use an Excalibur dehydrator and the non-stick liners are referred to as Paraflexx sheets.

If you don't have a dehydrator, don't worry. You can use a conventional oven on the lowest setting. Make sure to use the fan setting. Some people leave the door open while using the oven as most ovens' temperatures don't go as low as dehydrators. If you are leaving the oven door open, make sure not to leave it unattended.

A dehydrator is an amazing piece of equipment to have in your kitchen. Unlike an oven, you can leave it unattended.

Top-end dehydrators can be expensive, but if you're planning on using it regularly, they are worth the investment!

For the recipes in this book, dehydrate at 42°C.

### food processor

A food processor is the easiest way to chop, grate, mix and slice your ingredients. Different blades are used for different cuts. The most common is the S-blade. General chopping and mixing is done with the S-blade. For recipes like the Coleslaw and Spiced Red Cabbage, the slicing blade should be used.

## juicer

The easiest way to juice fruits and vegetables is to use a juicer. Even leafy greens and herbs can be used in a juicer. If using a centrifugal juicer for greens, it helps to put them in first followed by something 'wet' like an apple or cucumber.

If you are going to be doing a lot of juicing, a masticating juicer is ideal as it is powerful and can handle lots of juicing. However they are slower than a centrifugal juicer.

## nut milk bag

A nut milk bag is a fine mesh bag that is usually made of nylon with a drawstring for ease of use. A nut milk bag is the easiest and quickest way to separate the nut pulp from the milk. Once you have poured the unseparated nut milk into the bag, make sure to tighten the drawstrings before you start to "milk" the bag.

## spiralizer

A spiralizer is a simple tool that turns vegetables such as courgettes, sweet potatoes and carrots into fine noodles. There are a variety of spiralizer models which work well.

If you don't have a spiralizer you can use a potato peeler to create 'tagliatelli' or a sharp knife to create noodles.

# Glossary

**agave nectar**

Agave nectar, sometimes called agave syrup, is a naturally occurring sweetener derived from various species of the agave plant which grows throughout Mexico and South America. Its appearance and taste is similar to honey. Agave nectar has a low GI. As with any sweetener, even naturally occurring, agave nectar should be eaten in moderation.

**Buckwheaties**

Soak a 250 g bag of buckwheat overnight by placing the buckwheat in a bowl and covering with water. Drain the water off the next day and rinse. Leave the buckwheat in the bowl for a day, rinsing it in the evening and the following morning, allowing it to sprout. Place the sprouted buckwheat into a dehydrator overnight to dry. This makes your buckwheaties.

**chia**

Chia seeds are tiny black or white seeds that are part of the mint family. It is a rich source of omega 3, anti-oxidants and protein. It can be eaten as a seed, sprinkled on top of food, or soaked to make a meal. Chia prepared as a meal, like the Blackberry Chia Pudding recipe, has a very distinct texture. When serving chia for the first time on our retreat, I tell ladies that it's a bit like Marmite - you'll either love it or hate it. If you find that chia's texture is not to your liking, try sprinkling it on things like porridge or salad.

**coconut oil**

Classed as a superfood, virgin coconut oil is rich in medium chain fatty acids and has been used for centuries in Ayurvedic medicine to prevent and cure diabetes, viral infections, cardiovascular problems and is also used for its antibacterial properties.

**goji berries**

Goji berries are a bright orange-red berry commonly grown in north-central and western China. They are classed as a superfood as they are especially rich in beta-carotene, vitamin C, B1 and B2 and minerals, amino acids and antioxidants.

## lucuma powder

Lucuma powder is made from the Peruvian lucuma fruit. It is a natural sweetener with a rich caramel-like aroma and creamy texture. It is a high source of nutrients including beta-carotene, vitamin B3, iron, zinc, calcium, magnesium, and other vitamins and minerals.

## maca powder

Maca, grown in the mountains of Peru, is derived from a root that is related to the radish family. Maca is a versatile and amazingly nutrient packed food that benefits are numerous. Known as nature's Viagra, maca is beneficial to both men and women. In addition to increasing stamina and boosting libido, maca is particularly helpful for women by naturally balancing hormones.

## matcha tea powder

Matcha tea powder is green tea that has been ground into a powder. The health benefits of green tea are expansive, helping with everything from memory, concentration and anxiety plus it also helps detox your body.

## nori sushi sheets

Nori sheets are made from red sea-weed, dried and made into sheet form. Nori contains iodine, vitamin C and can also help you meet your daily needs for potassium, vitamin A and magnesium.

## nut milk

Almond milk is the most common nut milk due to its mild flavour. However, other nuts, such as Brazil nuts, can be turned into milk. High in anti-oxidants and nutrients, nut milk is a great replacement for cows' milk. Nut milk should be stored in an air-tight container in the refrigerator and will last about 3 to 4 days. It will separate while in the fridge, so just stir before use.

## probiotic capsules

Probiotic capsules are a health supplement used to maintain a healthy digestive system and they can be purchased in any health food store. The powder aids the fermentation process in recipes such as the Cashew Yoghurt. Make sure to use the powder within the capsule and dispose of the shell.

## psyllium husks

Psyllium husks are a soluble fibre used to aid general intestinal health. For the recipes in this book, use loose psyllium husk powder (not capsules).

## raw cacao butter

Raw cacao butter comes in creamy white coloured blocks and is extracted from raw cacao beans using a cold press method. It has a deep, sweet chocolate-like aroma and is naturally high in antioxidants.

## raw cacoa nibs

Cacao nibs are the unprocessed cocoa beans that are broken down into small pieces. They contain all the health benefits of raw chocolate and add texture and flavour to any dish.

## raw cacao powder

The advantages to raw cacao powder include: lowering blood pressure, improving circulation, neutralizing free radicals, promoting cardiovascular health, can aid digestion, suppressing appetite, is an aphrodisiac and it induces a great sense of wellbeing.

## rice mirin

Rice mirin is a type of Japanese rice wine.

## tahini

Tahini is a paste made from ground, hulled sesame seeds used in North African, Greek, Turkish and Middle Eastern cuisine.

## tamari

A type of Japanese soy sauce that doesn't contain wheat. It is dark in colour with a rich taste.

## tamarind concentrate

Tamarind has a unique sweet and sour flavour and is used extensively in South East Asian and Indian cooking. Tamarind is a seed pod and can be bought in a block form or as a concentrated paste that has had the seeds removed.

# Index